Stumbling
Toward Enlightenment

Stumbling
Toward Enlightenment

An Illustrated Crisis Companion

Barbara Lewis-Marco

A Perigee Book

Some of the images that appear in this book are
used by permission of Zedcor, Inc., Tucson, AZ,
from the 30,000-image DeskGallery® collection,
copyright © 1994 by Zedcor, Inc. 1-800-492-4567.

Clip art from "Clip Art Pro" used with permission
of Softkey International, Inc., copyright © 1994.

A Perigee Book
Published by The Berkley Publishing Group
A member of Penguin Putnam Inc.
200 Madison Avenue
New York, NY 10016

Copyright © 1997 by Barbara Lewis-Marco
Book design by Jackie Frant
Cover design by Joe Lanni
Cover illustration by Barbara Lewis-Marco

First edition: December 1997

Published simultaneously in Canada.

The Putnam Berkley World Wide Web site address is
http://www.berkley.com

Library of Congress Cataloging-in-Publication Data
Lewis-Marco, Barbara.
        Stumbling toward enlightenment : an illustrated crisis companion /
    by Barbara Lewis-Marco. — 1st ed.
                p.   cm.
        "A Perigee book."
        ISBN 0-399-52348-0
    1. Stress (Psychology)—Quotations, maxims, etc.   2. Crises—
    Psychological aspects—Quotations, maxims, etc.   3. Stress
    management—Quotations, maxims, etc.   I. Title
    BF575.S75L48   1997
    158—dc21   97-2304
                                                CIP

PRINTED IN THE UNITED STATES OF AMERICA

10   9   8   7   6   5   4   3   2   1

for
Jesse and Daniel

Part One

Stumbling into Crisis

didn't see it coming

why me?

the i can't handle it stage

the cry me a river phase

blaming someone

blaming yourself

raging at the gods

falling into despair

acceptance (reluctant)

acceptance (real)

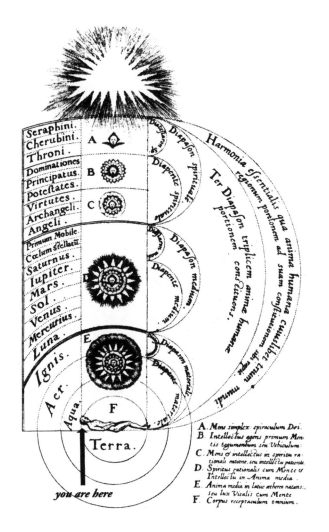

you are here

trying to trust in a divine plan

doubting there is one

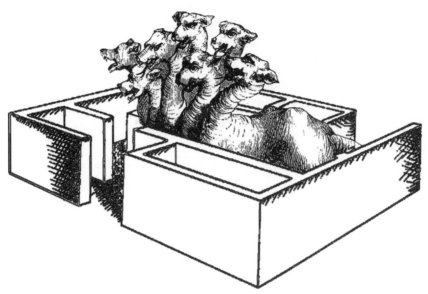

contemplating courage

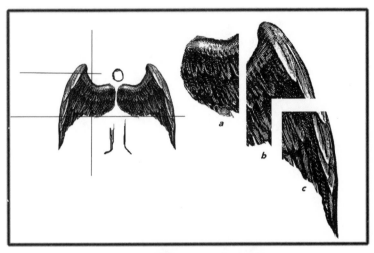

rising to the challenge

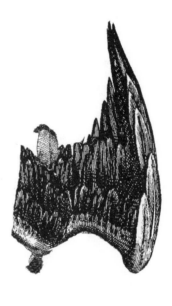

falling

getting yourself together

rising again

Part Two

Stumbling
into Daily Life

begin with a single step

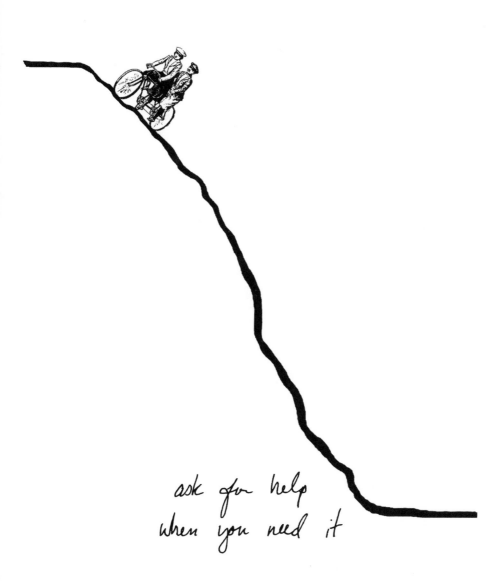

ask for help
when you need it

hang on to your sense of humor

appreciate small things

consciously
try to ^ orchestrate your life

be more compassionate toward yourself

be more compassionate toward others

be brave

ay out when necessary

try a different perspective

do the best you can

follow your heart

Part Three

Possible Pitfalls

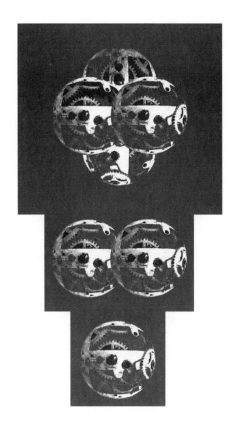

the mechanics of fear

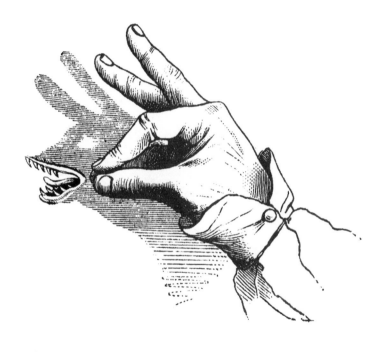

your shadow

Walls

impatience

ego

anger

attachment

control

Part Four

Stumblers' Wisdom

remember how pearls are made

appreciate the riddles
and paradoxes of life

adversity is fertilizer for growth

getting lost is part of the journey

the hand of fate may be quite imposing

try no judgment

RESPONS

responsibility is not a dirty word

reflect when it's hardest

consider forgiveness

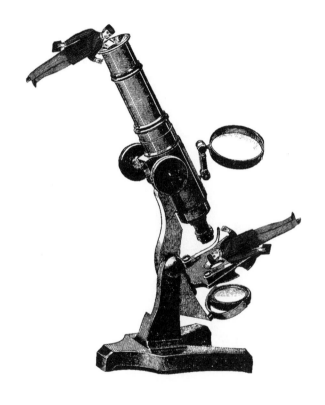

Know thyself

it's in your hands

impermanence rules

the gift is the present

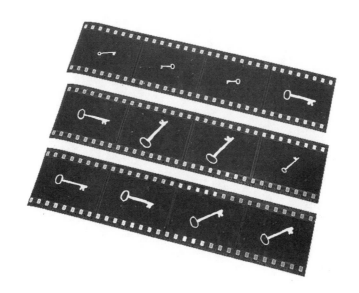

the image is not the key

expect the unexpected

it's all in the timing

remember to play

attend to your dreams

OFFICIAL STATEMENT

question reality

meditate for peace

nature is generous. be thankful

it really doesn't matter

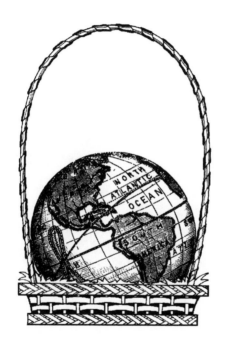

we're all in the same basket

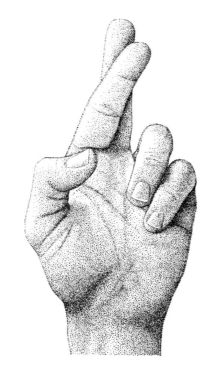

pray, in whatever forms you choose

serve, in whatever forms you choose

love, in whatever forms you choose